ANCHOR
BOOKS

WITTY WORDS

Edited by

Heather Killingray

First published in Great Britain in 1998 by
ANCHOR BOOKS
1-2 Wainman Road, Woodston,
Peterborough, PE2 7BU
Telephone (01733) 230761

HB ISBN 1 85930 635 7
SB ISBN 1 85930 630 6

FOREWORD

Anchor Books is a small press, established in 1992, with the aim of promoting readable poetry to as wide an audience as possible.

We hope to establish an outlet for writers of poetry who may have struggled to see their work in print.

The poems presented here have been selected from many entries. Editing proved to be a difficult task and as the Editor, the final selection was mine.

Many of us find humour an easy method of expressing ourselves, it is a particular quality we all love to see in a person. For those of us in hard times when we don't feel as if we can express humour ourselves, reading it always helps to produce a happier state of mind.

The commendable pieces of work within *Witty Words* all mean a great deal to the individual poets and they hope you can gain the feeling of the moment, as they can, when reading their poems.

Although this collection has a main theme running through it, there is a poem for every single one of us. Read it and find yours!

I trust this selection will delight and please the authors and all those who enjoy reading poetry.

Heather Killingray
Editor

CONTENTS

STEREOTYPE

Mass production people
Wearing mass production clothes
Smelling of mass production perfume
Getting up everybody's nose.

K Dickinson

THE D I Y ENTHUSIAST

So . . . Your chap is a D I Y Enthusiast . . .
Before you wed . . . some questions to be asked
When he's convinced there's a job that must be done
Are you prepared to be a *gofer* . . . It's no fun.

You may be relaxing at the end of the day
'We'd better start wallpapering again' he'll say
So . . . Are you willing in your spare time to begin
To strip those walls before your husband comes in?

You should always be one step ahead you know
As you'll be sent to look for lost tools, high and low
(You'll probably find them in a heap on the floor
And . . . only just inside, his workshop door.)

I think you'll find car repairs are the worst thing
Standing for hours in the cold, then find and bring
Tempers can get short when the weather's not kind
Tell me truthfully . . . will you really not mind . . . ?

The electrical jobs are a worry as well
As these chaps work 'Live' frightening to tell
Carpentry projects are a lot better to do
Watch out for nails and splinters . . . my advice to you.

Those plumbing repairs can be a nightmare
(Keep buckets handy as water flows everywhere)
It is the garden jobs which I like best of all
For these I am ready before hubby can call.

You will never need a builders estimate
Hubby can start now . . . he has no reason to wait
And his labour is cheap as no wages we pay
But . . . don't forget . . . who cleans up at the end of the day . . .

Valerie Ovais

HOME GROWN

I've read about the Wild West
Where the Sioux were mighty foes
But the red-skins that I like the best
Are still found on tomatoes.

D S Hussey

THE MOUSE

I have a little mouse
That lives in my house
I put out some cheese every night
Now she's bringing her brood
All looking for food
And my budget is getting so tight.

Cathie Bridger

MY DOG HONEY

My dog Honey begs for eggs.
My dog Honey loves cheese.
She'll even get down on her hands and knees
And say *Please!*

Melita Colton

STAN THE VAN

There lived, down our way, an old man called Stan
Who drove a classic fluorescent pink van
On fermenting cow pats, the old thing ran
And was subject to no EEC Regulations or ban

On his old van, Stan had painted a large nude
Subject to much comment, some said it was rude
It was in fact a young lady from Bude
Happy hunting ground of Stan where he was known as Jude.

He sold his old van to a vicar's wife
Who bleached it white
And old Stan died of shock
'Cause it just weren't right.

Clive Cornwall

DONCASTER SALMON

It was easy for him to become indispensable
To the river.
Green thigh length waders,
A practised casting of the rod,
Graceful and elegant line into the cold waters
Of the Tweed.
Green wax jacket and cap,
And knowledge of the salmon
That swam up the river each year.
No Scots accent,
I felt disappointed;
He spoke Yorkshire
And lived in Doncaster.
Hadn't caught a salmon
In thirty years of casting,
But loved them,
And was indispensable
To the river.
Enjoyment doesn't have to depend
On success!

Margaret Black

GOING TO CHURCH ON SUNDAY

The bells are calling the people in,
      'Come now and repent of your sin'
On this day of rest,
      dressed in their 'Sunday Best'.

Through the churchyard you pass
      ancient graves and stained glass.
Meeting friends, old and new
      on the way to your favourite pew.

Pause for a moment at the door,
      look at the brass rubbings on the floor.
Smell the flowers for a while
      then quickly move on down the aisle.

Slide along on polished wood
      where countless men of faith have stood.
In quiet reverence you wait,
      for the Rector and his Curate, (he's always late!)

Noisy children come in with a rush
      Till their mother tells them 'Shush!'
Every little girl and boy,
      God's own special 'bundle of joy'.

Now the Rector in robes white, red and green,
      can be seen.
The organ notes resound
      to hymns of praise all around.

On hassocks, kneeling, we pray
        for the world today.
Our sins we confess and devotion express,
        'You are forgiven' the Rector will say.
At his command, we stand
        and listen to God's Holy Word,
Read all the facts
        taken from Acts,
And wonderful Psalms can be heard.

Chalices of silver brightly shine,
        containing gifts of bread and wine.
At the alter we kneel at His feet,
        the Eucharistic Feast we take and eat.

We remember Him,
        who died for our sin.
There by the candle's flickering flame
        we thank Him again.

The sermon is too long and slow,
        to lunch you are waiting to go!
But listen for a message there to keep,
        stop that coughing, don't fall asleep!

The service is over, a wedding awaits,
        see the beautiful bride at the gates?
Please come again before you die,
        shake hands with the Rector - 'Goodbye'.

C M Kemp

PAVAROTTI

My mum loves Pavarotti -
I really don't know why.
Maybe it's his music,
Maybe it's his belly,
Or maybe when she sees him on the telly.

Laura Cation

FUNNY HA HA

Have a say, alive and well
Time for comedy, small wonders
It's art for fun's sake
Mix up over fun, Ha, Ha
Staff all set for wild time
Man found on Mars
Honest it's true
Man found on Mars
Believe me or not
Have a laugh, it's fun
Yes, man found on Mars
Well he was
He was standing on his Mars Bar
Well Ha, Ha, Ha
Man found on Mars, Ha, Ha, Ha
Mix up, laughter, have a laugh
Tell a joke, have a laugh
Have a say, alive and well
Two fish in a tank
Gilbert and George
Gilbert said to George after they swam round twice
Hey, look haven't we been here before
Ha, Ha, Ha
Yes, have fun, have a laugh
Tell a joke, it's fun
Comedy funny, Ha, Ha
Have a say, alive and well
Good times, take care
Have some fun
Join in, have a party.

David J Hall

WORDS FAIL ME

It had been a special holiday
Rendered more special yet
By the beauty of the location, so a poem was in order.

I thought long and hard,
Seeking a simile to convey my feelings.
Yet no sooner had I found it
Than it got up and walked away
Like, well, one of those things that walks away.

'Right,' I said to myself.
'You think you personify something, do you?
Well, if that's the way you want it,
So be it.'
But no sooner had I lured it, er, him, into place
Than it, he, whatever, refused to move, nor even breathe.

Exasperated, I sought a sound that would make it jump.
An explosion? A horrifically shrill scream?
Perhaps muttering inaudibly would gain its attention.
Unfortunately every noise seemed somehow inadequate.
Onomatopoeically mute, I tried another tack.

No more outflanking manoeuvres.
Time to adopt a new strategy,
Encompass it within a set of cunning tactics,
Capture it in my metaphorical trap.
But it would not be anything except itself.
Literally beautiful.

My last recourse was to look within.
What might my life, or that of all mankind, contain
That this stunning place could represent?
But I finally had to admit defeat when my symbols declared
'We're not standing for it!'
And stalked off into someone else's poem.

Colin Padgett

ALPHA TO OMEGA

A Beautiful, Callow,
Doe-Eyed Fawn
Grazes Hesitantly.

In Jeopardy.
Knows Lurking Man
Nearby, Out Poaching.

Quietly Runs
Swiftly Through Undergrowth.
Vanish Winsome Xenophobic!
Yield your Zone!

Anne Crofton Dearle

LAUGHTER IS A TONIC

They say, laughter is a tonic,
That keeps the doctor away,
So why not make changes in your life
And share a joke each day.

Listen to funny stories,
Also tell your own ones, too,
'Cos you'll find that others like listening,
To the stupid things you do.

So if you're always sad and gloomy,
And your friends are just the same,
It means none of you have a sense of humour,
So you've all got yourselves to blame.

Now some folk 'drown their sorrows',
And start to drink or smoke,
Whereas, it doesn't cost any money,
To listen, or tell a joke.

Jean Hendrie

CAPRICORN

My dad bought a goat
to keep in the garden
and save mum a fortune
in cheese and milk.
One day, while they were out,
it snuck in the house
and chewed up mum's curtains.
All of them.
So dad shot it.
And mum cooked it.
As we chewed up the goat,
we stared at the stars
through the curtainless windows;
never having noticed
them before.

Barbara L Richards

CARING

This wonderful caring society
Deserves treating with some sobriety,
Not sniffed at or laughed at don't you see,
Especially as it is caring for me!

Counsellors, carers, all in a row,
Now don't be anxious, you'll all get a go!
Lawyers will litigate, solicitors sue,
Isn't it nice they're all caring for you!

The ladies these days, they are ever so free,
I used to have several caring for me!
They've come a long way since Adam gave up his rib,
Now it's three hearty cheers for new Women's Lib!

Animals are cared for and liberated too.
I wonder if they prefer jungle or zoo?
Still, don't worry about that now, just set them free,
Then everyone can get back to caring for me!

Terry J Ward

UNTITLED

My name is Sam
When I grow up to be a man
I want to sail to China and Japan.
My name is Sadie
And when I grow up to be a lady
I want to get married and have a baby.
My name is Sam
And when I grow up to be a man
I want to give Sadie a baby
And to blazes with China and Japan.

Elizabeth Brown

UNTITLED

I get picked up,
I get put down.
I get dipped in the water and swished around.
I get rubbed and squeezed and put on a rope,
What am I?
      Soap.

Janet Scott

ACHOO!

There once was a girl named Sue,
who couldn't stop going achoo!
She sneezed so hard,
she ended up in Scotland Yard,
and said I didn't catch the bus, I flew!

Janice Tucker

OLD

Old as I am, old as I am
The mind will think I can
Legs won't work
Chair will irk
Why do I still think I can.
Ears fail
Voice can't hail
Head will think I can,
Forgetful too
Am I who?
Do you remember who I am.

Trish Birtill

ANCIENT GREEK

You may have heard that Socrates
Had knobbly knees.
That he had a snub nose
Everybody knows.

Nick Colton

DEAR MR...

Dear Mr ... ,
     This was new territory for me,
Much as the riverbank was for Moley.
The place was packed - I suddenly felt nervous.
You were taller than I imagined.
When you lounged in that chair, stretching your corduroy-clad legs,
You looked so relaxed you could have been at home.
(Orin Betty's Tea-rooms)

Dear Mr ... ,
     You looked younger than I expected.
('Course, the excitement and the complimentary wine were conspiring
to make me feel giddy).
I didn't have a question. (It's not often I have any answers either).
But I just wanted to leap up and say how happy I was to be there.
Of course, I didn't.
But I thought of a million things I could have said . . . on the way home.

Dear Mr ... ,
     Through your writing, I feel as if I know you -
Like a comfortable old cardigan. (But of course, I don't).
Thank you for making me awake of others.
You've made the conversations of ordinary folk, matter!
I climbed onto the platform. I'm sure I queued for days!
When you fixed me with those eyes, saying those magical words,
'Is it Karen with a *K*?' for one monumental moment, . . .
I couldn't remember.
I couldn't even feel the ground . . . Mr Bennett.

Karen E Barber

MY BIRTHDAY PARADE

'It's my Birthday Parade
I've a bit of a wheeze,
So I'll take my old rug
To cover my knees.'

'Just see if my phaeton
Is still down by the gate.
Please hurry up Philip
We're gonna be late.'

'I think mother's gone
As I heard a big cheer,
I bet all the Guardsmen
Were out on the beer.'

'Brigade Major's waiting
He's the one I call Gus,
If he can't catch his horse
There's always a bus.'

'Just look at the Guardsmen
Try to get them in line,'
'Where is my umbrella?'
'I hope it stays fine.'

'One more parade over,'
'Shall I give them a wave?'
'Then hot fish and chips mate
That I've told Bill to save.'

'Is my balcony clean?'
'Charlie swept it of course,'
'Thank goodness I didn't
Have to ride my old horse!'

Peter James O'Rourke

LUCKY

I've tried to win my fortune,
So I could be rich and have it all,
Since I met that lady,
With her little crystal ball,

'I can see a stranger,'
She said will a little grin,
'He's holding lots of money,
Chanting win, win, win,'

So I've tried the pools, horses and lottery,
Putting my luck to the test,
And ten pounds for three numbers,
Is so far my very best,

It seems as though my luck is out,
Perhaps it's not supposed to be,
But I'll carry on without a doubt,
Because one day it could be me!

John Willard

HIGHWAYMAN

Behind the mask
He expected the coach
Hearing hooves
He saw it approach
'Stand and Deliver'
He shouted the command
When it stopped
He issued his demand
They stepped out
He saw her face
She just smiled
He knew her place
'I've no money'
He said 'Your life'
The man bargained
He took his wife.

Michael A Leonard

MY MUM BERYL AND HER FAITHFUL DUSTER

If ever you're in Brixton
I hope you'll take great care
Especially if you see some dust
Go flying through the air.
It could be just the dustman
A car or just a bike
Or even some young kiddies too
Upon their little trikes.
But if you cannot see someone
Perhaps you then would find
The dust you see is coming from
A house that you're beside
So just in case this happens
I'll tell you what to do
As then you won't feel frightened
If a duster follows you.
First of all jump up and down
Then turn yourself around
Clap your hands and stamp your feet
Real hard upon the ground.
But now a word of warning too
Whatever you all do
Never pause a moment
You'll regret it if you do.
As out will pop my special mum
With duster in her hand
And then she'll try to polish you
As quickly as she can.

Merilyn Gulley

THE DINNER-LADY'S RETIREMENT

No more tears in the carrots,
Now that Sheila has gone,
Or lumps in the custard,
Or pud that's well done.

No more bacon that shatters,
Or bangers that bounce,
Or rice pud like Bostik,
That sticks to your mouth.

No more dumplings like dumbbells
And mince that's like grit,
Or cabbage that tastes
Like it's come out the pit.

No more chips and fish fingers
That are burnt to a turn,
For Sheila has gone home,
No more to return.

Marian Hamilton

WITCH HAZEL

Scatty Hazel a silly witch
Rides too high on her old broomstick
Over rooftops, over trees
Clutching the broom between her knees.

Looking such a frightful sight
Black against the pale moonlight
Swooping up and swooping down
Over the silent sleeping town.

Up she goes higher and higher
Way above the old church spire
Circling like a huge black crow
Over the rooftops far below.

Singing a wild and wonderful tune
She flew three times around the moon
Then noticed a big black hairy spider
Sitting on the broom beside her.

It gave her such a nasty scare
She lost her balance and fell through the air
Down she came faster and faster . . .
Knowing she was heading for disaster
She quickly waved a magic wand . . .
And landed in a huge blancmange!

Eileen Bailey

DEATH OF A POEM

I am struggling with this poem
so did not hear you call.
Yes, I do know Richard's muddy boots
are on the carpet in the hall.

There is a heron in the fishpond,
so, chase it away.
I thought it ate all the fish
the day before yesterday.

Of course dinner is not ready
put that biscuit tin away.
Turn the television down,
yes, you may go out to play.

I know the tap is leaking
I told you yesterday.
Pull the plug out of the basin
so the water runs away.

The milkman wants his money
the washing up can wait.
The car has got a flat
so your Mum and Dad are late.

The dog has done what,
where did you say.
I was struggling with a poem
now I think it's gone away.

Take that horrid frog away . . .

Jean Gabrielle Gillings

THE NIGHT THE BOGEY-MAN FLICKED MY EAR

On Hallowe'en the witches flew
over cauldrons of bubbling brew.
Slimy goblins teased and taunted
bright white ghosts hovered and haunted.
But nothing could compare with the fear
of the night when the bogey-man flicked my ear.

Sound asleep, I knew no dread
as his arm arose from beneath my bed
finger poised, then into gear
he lined it up then flicked my ear.
Mummy, I screamed, oh mummy dear
how could you let him get so near.
From under my bed he begins to jeer.
So mummy, startled, kicked his rear.

Battered, bruised and rubbing his bum,
that's the last time he'll mess with my mum.
Hiding his eyes from the light of the day,
he leaves no trace as he scuttles away,
no proof of his visit, no slimy trail,
just mummy and me to tell our tale.

Kay Baker

THE GNOME'S LAMENT

I am a little garden gnome,
I sit here day and night
With fishing rod beside the pond -
But never get a bite.

The other gnomes beside me hold
Wheelbarrow, lantern, spade,
And all of us stuck in the sun
And never in the shade.

The paint peels off our hats and coats,
And off our faces too,
And as for dogs - well you know dogs
And what they like to do!

It isn't fun to be a gnome -
The birds perch on my nose,
The spiders dangle from my chin
And snails crawl round my toes.

In winter time I'm frozen stiff
With snow up to my knees,
At other times the rain beats down -
Someone take pity please.

It isn't nice to spend one's life
Out in the cold and wet,
Please take me into your warm home
And treat me like a pet!

Eleanor Rogers

IF

If there wasn't any money
Wouldn't life be funny?
What a ball we could have
And life would be
One great laugh.
If there was no-one ever ill
There'd be no need
To take a pill.
If there wasn't any food
There'd be no pots to dry
If I wasn't in the mood.
If there were no schools
Who would need to obey rules?
No trees
No skies
No birds
Or flies.
No stars
Or cars
No strife -
No life!

Heidelind Howell

MUDDY CATS

Cats with a glaring angry growl,
who stalk through the night on graceful prowl,
flick their large muddy paws,
and make a mess on kitchen floors.
House-proud owners don't like the sight
of chewed up carpet now black not white.

Kirsten Mellows

GOING FOR THE BIG TIME

A cellist, Magnolia Pride
Had hips that were not very wide
Her limited straddle
Meant playing side-saddle
Instead of the usual astride.

So in order to conquer this riddle
She devised stretching games for her middle
Now her problem is solved
And a new self evolved
That can cope with a full-sized bass fiddle.

Joe Silver

HOW NICE TO BE PLACID!

How nice to be placid
and not to care
if a family of bats
makes nests in your hair.

How nice to let insults
bounce off your back;
to smile at the bully
you long to smack!

How nice to be pleased
with yourself and your actions,
oblivious to rivals
and similar factions.

I wish I could be it
I really do,
but placid I can't be
even for you!

Geraldine Squires

MARRIAGE

My husband - he is perfect - or as near as one can get.
I've worked for 40 years on him, I've not quite finished yet.
The jobs not been an easy one, we've worked hard at it - you see
It's taken hubby just as long - to make a perfect wife of me.

D Gallard

THE JOYS OF FIFTY

My mum-in-law, Jackie, has just hit the big *five 'O'*
It's now time to let herself go.
Forget the make-up to enhance yourself,
Go on, feel free to let it hang out.

You could try if you liked all those potions and creams,
To firm up those bits that aren't to be seen,
You could cover the wrinkles and hide the grey hair,
But in the end you'd know that it's still there.

So after some thought, I think you'll agree,
The decision is as easy as one, two, three,
So let the grey show from the roots, an extra pound well who
                                        gives a hoot
Don't bother worrying about saggy skin,
It's all down hill so grab a gin.

Jane Harrison

JUST DESSERTS
(Based on a story told by my daughter Andrea to her baby sister)

I bought a pack of jelly-babies
And took them to my home.
I took them to my bedroom
So I could eat them on my own.
The packet I then opened
And gave a mighty shout,
As a jelly-baby jumped from it
And started scampering about.
It said it was escaping,
It wasn't ready to be eaten.
I tried to catch it quickly
But I was well and truly beaten.
The naughty jelly-baby
Ran across the bedroom floor.
I jumped up and ran after it
But it made it through the door.
Then down the stairs it bounded
Laughing loud with glee
Throwing up its jelly arms
Delighted to be free.
It raced around the living room,
And scuttled past a chair.
As it headed for the kitchen
I yelled, 'No, don't go in there.'
But too late, the kitchen beckoned,
And the door was open wide.
The jelly-baby vanished
So I followed it inside.
Of the naughty jelly-baby
I could not find a trace,
But my big dog was sitting there
With a huge smile on his face.

Jan Lingard

ALL IS NOT GOLD

In a little cottage garden
Near a place called Giggleswitch
Was where my dear old Granddad
Once thought he'd struck it rich.

Whilst hoeing through his onions,
Weed shifting by the ton,
He chanced upon a golden ring
A-glinting in the sun.

With happy cry 'Eureka,
'At last I have it made'
He rushed down to the goldsmith
To have his find assayed.

The goldsmith took one look at it
He didn't need his lab,
His words near broke my Granddad's heart
'It's from a sherbet dab.'

Alf Godman

THE MERRY WIDOWS

Four buxom ladies of eighty three
Widows all 'tis plain to see,
Enjoy their fill of liberty,
They've never felt so free,
Accepting life right merrily;
Oh what lucky souls are we
They exclaim so very lustily,
They think it is so heavenly
To drink their morning cup of tea,
And continue very doggedly
With all their widowed jollity,
And live they hope till ninety three,
Then continue in eternity
To sip etheric cups of tea!

Eric Allday

EXPECTATIONS

I don't believe in fairies
But mum says it's the truth
They will leave you out some money
If you leave them a tooth.
I've got one rather wobbly
So I wriggle it about
And joy of joys - a little tug
It's out - it's out - it's out.
It's underneath my pillow
Before I go to sleep
I can't wait for the morning
When I can have a peep
Coo! - A shiny fifty pence piece
And a twenty pence one too
I do believe in fairies
I do - I do - I do!
And I've got lots more teeth here
So I pull with all my might
But I'm so disappointed
'Cos they're tight - they're tight -they're tight
I know! - I've got an idea
I'll get rich - I'll be bound
For underneath my pillow
Dads false choppers can be found

Irene Beattie

THE GARDEN

To 'do' the garden
Is relaxing they say.
Can someone please tell me,
Have I missed my way?

I'm out in all weathers
Soaked to the skin.
I've got nettle rash,
Where I didn't know the nettles got in!

Am I doing it all wrong?
Please give me a clue,
If it keeps on like this
I'm concreting all through.

A E Bentley

ADMONITION TO A LEAD-LOVING DOG

A lead, I've told you, is a badge
Of servitude. No self respecting dog
Should want a lead. Just look
At what is on the other end!
(Well, sometimes, anyway.)
But saying that you feel half dressed
Without a lead is quite absurd.
I *know* it's walkie wear for lots of dogs
And lots of dogs deserve it too,
But only those who tend to wander off.
A collar, now, well, that's a different case.
Your collar is a passport. It's the sign
That you belong, and where your medals hang.
You say the law is on your side. But then,
The law does not concern itself with fields and tracks
And country dogs who rarely see a street.
But should you ever find yourself
Caught by the law for leadlessness in town
Be sure that I will stick by you and plead
That you be let off charge and lead.

Bill Johnson

SCAREDY CAT

It was a fine, dry October day,
The first for quite a while.
The cat was in the garden
Sitting on the stile.

I watched her from the window,
She was content to be outside.
Then, suddenly, she ran indoors,
Big eyes opened wide.

I knew that she was frightened,
As she crouched low to the ground.
I wondered what had startled her,
When I heard an unusual sound.

How can I best describe it?
A sort of thud and then two clicks,
Followed by a shopping trolley's wheels,
As they turn upon the bricks.

I went outside to take a look
Such a sight I had never seen
The road was lined with 'sentry pairs'
In brown and olive green.

A voice from nowhere then piped up
And tells me that he feels
That I will like this council scheme
Of dustbins upon wheels.

I placed ours in the garden.
We'll need a bigger nook.
It didn't take young puss long
To come and have a look.

She leapt onto the top of one,
I knew that's what she'd do.
She sat up straight and miaowed at me,
'Mum, I'm as tall as you.'

Sue Jenner

PIG-HEARTED

The medical profession is planning ahead
To keep us alive when we all should be dead
A male chauvinist who thinks he is big
May soon trot around with the heart of a pig
Middle-aged, pot-bellied, he's wondering how
He'll ever keep up with his dynamic sow
For tho' menopausal she's on HRT
The 'litter's' left home and it's *'time to be me'*
She's not contented cooped up in the 'sty'
The world's opening up - she can see the blue sky
She just wants to breathe where the air is like wine
And not spend her days dishing dirt with some swine
For sure in the 90's it's really no joke
To wake up and feel like a pig in a poke
If her hair starts thinning she won't give a fig
Should nature ravish, she'll just don a wig
There's so much to do and so little time
Babe, she's not joking, she's just reached her prime
She wants to be living, not looking ahead
To a time when they're old or possibly dead
She's no time for a pig with a soft curly tail
Or wandering around at the pace of a snail
She wants to be living and loving and bedded
By a man with a heart - tho' he might be *pig-headed*

M A Rogan

My Doctor Said

Oh my God, Mrs Hunt is here again
Each time she comes it's another pain
I'll give her some tablets, I know all the tricks
One day soon though, I'll try 'pick and mix'
I have to give her antibiotics, she doesn't want to cough,
Always afraid she says, of something dropping off.
First it's her blood pressure, then it's her heart.
You would never believe, that's only the start
I have to listen too, about the ringing in her ears
That has been a problem for quite a few years
She is going deaf, has a deformed toe
Something wrong all over, nowhere else to go.
Get yourself undressed now, I'll take a look at you.
But really I would rather not, I don't enjoy the view
The patient is a long time behind that flipping curtain,
Just take a look nurse, we have to be quite certain
She may have gone to sleep, sometimes she does do that
She is sound asleep, while here I am sat
Wake up my dear, no you're not in Heaven
You're in the doctor's surgery down here in Devon.
Make your next appointment on your way out
And please, wear your hearing aid, then I won't have to
Shout.

Joan Jeffries

DECEIVER'S EVER

Cleopatra was angry with Ceasar,
who had made an attempt to deceive her.
He was caught with a maid,
but said, 'Dear, I'm afraid
that I thought you had said 'Julius seize her.''

Grace Mills

THE TRIALS OF A FOUR-YEAR-OLD

I'm trying to put the dog on a lead
With Dad's striped tie from someone called Hermes
And he's not pleased
Nor is the dog.

I'm busy using the plane like Dad
Planing the fridge making grooves and channels
But that doesn't work
I've scraped the enamel.

I'm trying to mix a cake like Mum
Stirring lots of eggs in a lemon curd jar
It's cracked,
There's glass all over the floor.

I'm refusing to eat Sunday lamb roast
As it's Mary's lamb and follows her
Wherever she goes
So the nursery rhyme says.

I'm building a tower with packets like bricks
But they're Dad's duty free cigarettes
Whatever that means
And he's angry.

I'm giving up learning for watching television
And Mum's going crazy
Out in the kitchen
The fish tank is full of felt tips!

Jan Ingram McCaffery

TEETHING PROBLEMS

She was only a Mundesley Mawther
Whose teeth were a bit of a pain
Oft poor dentist many times did she bother
Again and again, and again.

We'll fill up this little old hole here
And polish those there on the left,
Of good molars the really sad thing is
Her mouth was now almost bereft.

Back tooth is looking a bit shaky
And front one is way past its best
That one on the side I'm afraid Miss
I think it's as bad as the rest.

I have to say as I work with my drill here
There's not much good in this poor little mouth
There's sharp edges, worn molars and great gaps
And your wisdom's are all pointing south!

Now she'd dreaded this visit to dentist
But things are not half as bad as they seem
'Tis true the teeth are a bit motley
But he's given them a jolly good clean.

The staff are considerate and kind too
Ever helpful and welcoming me,
So 'fangs' for the memory - I must say
My fangs aren't what they used to be!

Mollie D Earl

TALKING JAZZ

One sunny afternoon, while sitting in the barber's chair,
I was asked the usual question as to how I'd like my hair.
So I told the man I'd like it off the ears and round the collar -
And before I even knew it, he was mentioning Fats Waller.

And so twenty minutes floated by, as we exchanged the pearls
Of the sable kings of melody - the Counts, the Dukes, the Earls -
Charlie Parker, who could write and play just like a bird in flight;
And Art Tatum, of whom Fats once said, 'God's in the house tonight.'

Now I'm woefully short-sighted, and he went a bit berserk,
As I found out when I donned my specs to scrutinise his work,
Recognised Mahatma Gandhi - but no way would I complain -
Knowing that, in six month's time, we'd be discussing John Coltrane.

Stephen Rudgwick

SURPRISE, SURPRISE!

'Young' Peter wrote off to 'Blind Date'
To find himself the perfect mate,
'Please can I be on your show?
I'm such a handsome hunk you know.'
They wrote back, they were impressed
'Come along and be well dressed.'

He was nervous just like a boy
Being picked would give much joy,
He wore trousers a size too small
And platform shoes to make him tall,
Then donned a wig of golden thatch
To hide his large and balding patch.

As he tottered onto the stage
He felt like he was all the rage,
People clapped and gave a cheer
Some even offered him a beer.
With floral shirt and kipper tie
Surely he'd be given the eye,

But when sitting down upon the chair
It collapsed and he lost his hair.
The lads were asked questions galore
Peter replied from down on the floor,
The unseen girl chose number three
A voice below said, 'Gosh, that's me.'

He crawled forward on his knees
'Sorry Cilla, forgive me please,
It seems that this is not my day'
And as the screen was drawn away,
He got the shock of his whole life
For there before him stood his wife!

Maureen Daniel

CORNY LOVE

When as in silks my Julia goes
rings on her fingers and corns on her toes.
Gliding along in her usual sweet way
'Good riddance to bad rubbish' I always say.
Behind her she'd leave a lingering smell
a wash certainly needed; she probably couldn't tell.
She walked like a woman always in pain
or maybe with too many men she had lain.
But my dear Julia, how I love her so
I'd love her till death, if only she'd *go*.
Then I'd cherish my cherub, my flowers, my rose
when as in silks my Julia, *goes*.

Esther Austin-Buah

VIEWING TIME AT THE ZOO

I think it is another day
When we can view those men.
You know, the animals they say
Who can even count to ten.

They say they're descended from the ape,
And you really must agree,
As they turn and stare and gape
It does look like their pedigree!

They push some titbits through our cage,
And can't then understand
And really get into a rage,
If we don't take it from their hand.

I really thought that they could read.
As there's a notice big and bold,
Saying 'Don't give the animals any seed,'
you would have thought they hadn't been told!

But really it is quite a treat.
You see - they are so funny,
It is a show you cannot beat,
And well worth anyone's money.

They scream and shout and jump about,
Licking ice-cream cones;
The gear and music that they flout
Is like swarming bees' drones.

I wonder if they find us fun,
As we do enjoy their visits,
Perhaps we should give *them* the odd bun
Or some of our nice titbits!

Beatrice Wilson

THE ADVENTURES OF SPLAT

'Splat' used to be a donkey
With long ears and a hat,
Full of woolly stuffing
That made him look quite fat.

But I put him in the washing machine
And sent him for a spin.
He ended up with half a tail,
And a very lopsided grin.

Mum left him on the line to dry
Hanging by his ear.
The sparrows pecked his stuffing out,
Which made him look quite queer.

One day I took him to the park
Where on a bench he sat.
Then a big fat lady sat on him.
So now I call him 'Splat!'

Gwen Hoskins

COVERED ONLY IN CONFUSION

We have a friend who's a teacher,
With the class he went on a trip,
The weather was warm,
He slept right through a storm,
So the class thought they'd give him 'the slip'.

On the town they went that night
And they drank local beer!
They came home in noisy state,
Started singing by the gate
Then all let out one loud and raucous cheer.

For our friend had gone to meet them
And ran out at such great speed
He forgot he was undressed
And with good portions he'd been blessed
So what a sight they did behold -
Oh what a sight indeed!

Gwen Daniels

DREAM OF INFINITY

I set out on an infinite journey
And travelled at infinite speed;
Believe me, I saw Einstein's grandma,
Just a blur, dressed in fur boots and tweed.

Time went backwards as I travelled forwards
And the past was as clear as a bell,
I saw Jacob, who said for ten shekels
He'd let me see Moses as well.

But I had to decline his kind offer
'Cause I only just had fifty pence
And not knowing the going exchange rate,
To haggle just didn't make sense.

So I sped on and kept my eyes open:
I saw men who were savage and vicious,
And a woman without any clothes on
Who was holding a Golden Delicious.

Very soon I saw birds without feathers,
Their shrieks made a hideous chorus,
As they swooped down and pecked at the bottom
Of what looked like a young brontosaurus.

I got all depressed at this juncture,
So to keep up my spirits I sang,
Then I fell down a black hole at high speed
And woke up with one hell of a bang.

Roy Donoghue

THE ONSET OF RIGOR MORTIS (OR BORED STIFF!)

Here lies the body of Danny Kember,
   lifeless, nay! Deceased.
Stricken down quite rigid
   (but at last, a merciful release.)
Prostrate on the mortuary slab,
   staring with those vacant eyes,
as the coroner begins an inquest
   into his demise.
The autopsy report shall read;
   'The shedding of this mortal coil
has been due to apathy,
   from the work that is life's toil.'
The examiner's diagnosis,
   found by the post-mortem,
will reveal the cause of death
   to be from terminal boredom!

Danny Kember

THE CREAKING GATE

'How is your wife?' the vicar asked.
'Oh - not too well,' the husband sighed,
'With lots of rest, she should improve.'
'We'll pray for her,' the Rev replied.

Another Sunday morning came.
His partner couldn't sit for long.
'Her back is bad,' the husband said,
'But may be right by Evensong.'

Another weary week passed by.
The vicar prayed about the wife.
'She's ill again,' the husband said,
'Perhaps she will be sick for life!'

'Oh, vicar, would you pray for her?
If only we could heal her chest.'
The vicar smiled, uneasily.
The anxious husband beat his breast.

The church prayed on, persistently.
All healing prayers, the wife defied.
The 'creaking gate' lived on for years.
The healthy husband upped and died.

Pauline Pullan

STORMY WEATHER

The wind howls round the chimney tops
The rain is lashing down,
Umbrellas blowing inside out
All around the town.

Roads flooding now because the drains
Just cannot take more water.
Cars go past and drench my legs
At a speed they didn't oughter!

A rooftop tile barely misses
A gleaming Ford Fiesta,
The clouds scud dark across the sky
 - Oh for a summer siesta!

Water in my conservatory
The pond's near overflowing,
The lady on the telly says
More storms our way are blowing.

And you can bet the extra rain
Is rushing to the sea,
And in summertime the water board
Bans hoses for you and me.

Although they charge us more each year
They simply don't conserve
The flooding rain that's coming down,
They'll speak of drought - the nerve!

Anyway, there's one sure thing,
We cannot change the weather,
So we'll grin and bear it while it lasts,
It can't go on forever!

For the Lord has promised
Not to flood the world again
And has given a sign, the rainbow,
Which shines in sun and rain.

Joan Marsh

CATASTROPHE

I remember it was Friday when the problem first occurred -
I turned the bathroom taps on, and a knocking could be heard.
So I telephoned a plumber and was horrified to hear
That he was very busy till the start of the New Year!
Since it was only August now, I panicked quite a bit;
This knocking sound would send us mad if we couldn't get rid of it!

Well, we turned off all the water, and we fiddled with the pipes;
We turned the taps on, turned them off (we're not DIY types).
We didn't know what else to do, so we turned the water on -
And all the lights in the house went off! Whatever had we done?
We phoned the electrician, and he came within the hour,
And promptly turned the 'lectric off, then left us without power!

For seven days we struggled, couldn't wash or have a drink;
Couldn't cook or watch the telly, use the loo, the bath or sink.
In the end we called the council - Was there something they could do?
So they sent out an inspector and a fleet of workmen too!
Well, they drilled and poked and hammered from the roof down
                                          to the floor,
They made such an awful noise, I couldn't stand it any more!

So I took myself out shopping in a state of near despair,
And when I came back later, the Fire Brigade were there!
My house was full of bubbles, looking just like crazy foam;
It seemed the workmen had set fire to my poor beleaguered home!
Now we're staying in a hotel whilst our home they do restore,
And yes, we found the knocking sound - it was coming from next door!

Pauline Hepple

THE VISIT

'Good morning Doctor,' that's what I said.
'How can I help you?' through glasses he peered.
'I am suffering bad with a pain just here,
Though sometimes it leaps and lands just there.'

'Let's have a wee look,' then out with the book
He read and read until he stopped with a very grave stare.
His eyes looked so bright as I sat there.

'Oh Doctor is it serious?' you need to declare
For I want to get home, I feel in despair.
'Don't worry my dear, there is nothing to fear
All you need is right here.'

A long prescription he started to write
'Is it my kidney or liver Doctor?'
Just tell me please
'Or maybe I got a draught in the breeze.'

'Listen to me there are only three things it could be
So to be safe I will give for all three.'
'Oh Doctor that is wonderful, your service is grand,
But I forgot to say I have a pain in my hand.'

Hazel Wilson

WHICH BANK?

With pride I walked into my bank
At once my spirit quickly sank
Naked I stood, a sight to be seen
Thank God it was just a horrible dream.

Olive Bedford

SCROOGE (AT CHRISTMAS)

The family round the table sat
At dinner time on Christmas day,
And all eyes looked intently at
The food, that on the table lay.

Hot stuffing, sprouts, and spuds in piles.
The turkey though was rather small.
The children lost their happy smiles
When Dad said 'There's not enough for all!'

But Dad declared 'I will be fair.
Instead of you kids getting meat,
Here's fifty pence each for your share:
There's lots of spuds and greens to eat.'

When later on the table stood,
Like a whale washed up on a beach,
A huge steaming Christmas pud -
The kids got fifty pence worth each!

Jack Judd

THE ENTERTAINER

The festival was well on the way,
The clowns were here and the jugglers too,
Floods of people were arriving now.
The entertainer I'd hired was still not here,
Panic, panic where could he be?
All of a sudden I got quite a shock,
A man ran onto the stage and dropped his pants,
The audience just laughed and cheered.
This was not the kind of act I'd planned.
'I think there's been a mistake' he said,
'I'm no entertainer' - his face now bright red.
I heard the message 'bare all £1.00 for charity'
I couldn't help grinning to myself,
So I paid him the entertainer's fee,
I hadn't the heart to tell him the truth!
The message was 'beer all £1.00 for charity'.

Barbara Lynch

DEAR PSYCHIATRIST

I think I'm going slightly mad
I'm doing silly things
I jumped out of the window
And thought that I had wings.
Then I put the kettle on
It didn't look too nice.
It didn't seem to suit me much
I ask for your advice.
Then I put the telly on
It was much too big in size.
I tried to get it on my head.
It seemed to hurt my eyes.
Then I went to make my bed.
The wood was much too long.
I never had enough large screws
It took me all day long.
Am I going slightly mad
Or can you give me hope
Will I ever be all right
Or always be a dope.
Can I leave my brains to science
I'm a voluntary donor.
You can tell the lucky person
That they only had one owner!

Irene Harrington

IT'S PANTO TIME!

Now once again it's panto time
The show is drawing near
The cast have all rehearsed their parts
And first night nerves are clear.

The electrician is on standby
Queuing in his lights
The fairy godmother's in a panic
He's laddered his spangled tights!

At this the tempers are fraying
Just like poor Cinder's dress
This was to be our opening night
And now it's just a mess.

But here's the dame and ugly sisters
With them we'll have some fun
For the curtain is now opening . . .
The show it has begun.

The audience are all laughing
They pick up every joke
For here is Baron Hardup
Admitting he's stony broke.

The poor old thing's so sad
He really doesn't have a clue
So he seeks out Buttons and Snow White
To ask them what to do.

They tell him to be happy
The audience start to clap
And on stage next comes Bonny
That clever horse can tap!

Oh how the crowd is roaring
But all too soon somehow
The cast is all lined up
To take a final bow.

Karen Sandiford

A WET KISS

Sitting on a lily pad enjoying summer's air,
Sat an ordinary garden frog, contentedly unaware,
For just across the water sat a royal little miss,
Puckering her cherry lips, to blow a little royal kiss,
It landed on his temple, and much to her surprise,
A young and handsome, noble prince, stood before her eyes.
He puzzled at his fancy clothes, his head so newly crowned,
But the lily pad refused the weight, the poor lad sadly drowned.

Jayne Wakefield

IT MAKES US LAUGH

Humour is very important to everybody in the street
From Tiny Tim in music hall days, balancing on gigantic feet.
The delightful genius of Ken Dodd
brought tears to my eyes and it hurt
His protruding teeth, soothing ballads
and the catchphrase . . . 'Where's Me Shirt?'
Morecome and Wise. Little and Large. The Chuckle Brothers too
Listening to Stanley Holloway on disc
'Yon Lion's Eaten Albert' at the zoo.

Jim Davidson. Russ Abbot. Freddie Starr.
Jethro, Julian Clary and Popeye
are among the funniest people it seems
that make us laugh till we cry . . .?

Charlie Chaplin was king of them all
never said a word for years
But his sad pathetic character was great
and we wept when he shed his tears.

Laughter is so varied a theme
as diverse as our British weather
No matter what the time or where it is . . .
Making people laugh is extremely clever.

John Ernest Day

HOPPING MAD!

Ouch! I sprout a growing lump,
A red and swelling painful bump.
I grab a hissing growling cat,
and search in vain around the mat.

To find a most elusive flea,
That's chosen for its next meal me!
Panic now surrounds the house
Search for spray to kill the louse.

Spray fills the room with noxious fumes,
While innocent that moggy grooms.
'It wasn't me' he seems to say,
'I'll go out till it's gone away.'

But he is next - just in case,
Around the house behind I chase.
Liberally sprayed he goes free.
I hope I killed that vicious flea!

Anne Jones

DIDDLEY SQUAT
(Dedicated to daughter Maura)

I knew a man called Diddley Squat,
His wife was Diddley Doo.
He had a son named Diddley Bat
And a daughter Diddley Boo.

They lived in a house named Diddley Dive,
In a road called Diddley Dong.
The town was Diddley Ditis
In the land of Diddley Wong.

They had a cat named Diddley Dum
Whose ears were diddley day
His tail was diddley double
And his colour diddley grey.

Diddley Squat was always diddling
For a firm of diddlers fine
And as a hobby after work
He diddled all the time.

Well, then at last, the Diddler Squat
Was called to a spot on high
And asked to account for his diddling
And this he did say in reply;

'All my life I've been a diddler
From baby, boy to man.
I've diddled in some far off sites
And in the Isle of Man.
But if you ask me 'what is diddling?'
I'd have to tell you true
I haven't got the foggiest
So diddley bye to you!

Joe Hughes

A Day In The Life Of A Glass Eye

'He sticks me in this sweaty hole
That's snug and warm and deep
With little bits of brain and things
Like crunchy bits of sleep,
I'm sure he's daft, but I'm not sure
It seems he is to me
I get this vague impression that
He thinks that I can see,
Sometimes he's rough and shoves me in
Just like he prods his ears,
It makes me feel like crying, but
I can't make any tears;
The high point of my day is when
He tries to scoop me out
I could be just a maggot, or
A plastic Brussel sprout;
He hacks, attacks and picks and pokes
I wish he'd die, or stop,
Though suddenly I'm free, it makes
This horrid squelch and 'plop',
I spend the night beside his bed
In noisy dingy drawers,
I'd rather be inside his head
Than listen to his snores;
If I could roll away, I would
But part of me is kind
Glass eyes are so misunderstood
Perhaps because they're blind!'

Nicholas Winn

THINGS THAT GO BUMP IN THE NIGHT

Four wee little ghosties learning how to scare
and turning a dream into a waking nightmare.
They hover with ease and create a chill breeze,
lifting dust mites that make you shiver and sneeze.
A rap on the door and a creak on the stairs
that brings up the goose bumps and raises your hairs.
They flicker the lights with aplomb and abandon,
moving objects of fancy from places at random.
Through walls they can walk with alacrity and ease
and fade in and out of view just to tease.
It's an atmosphere of fear that they plot and scheme
created by hollow manic laughter followed by a scream.
They use all of their wiles and all of their wails,
fear, dread and horror is all that prevails.
To frighten poor souls is their only desire,
to graduate in terror is to what they aspire.
Just remember to breathe and not hold on to your breath
for it's thrills that they're after not anyone's death.
So fear not the cold or the echoes and rattles
but remember your crosses, bell, book and candles.

Jean Selmes

THE DRIVER

My adoring eyes would catch him every day
In the heart of London town,
Cutting through the warming, busy streets
Driving up, down, and all around.
And I with deliberation would stand on the
corner by a teashop,
Pretending to be looking on, yet I yearned
for him to come, and stop.
But if my tiresome feet should never lose
their direction, nor falter,
For as I remember it, 'twas my desire for him
to lead me to the sacred alter!
Then one fine morning I boarded his black cab
and his voice was so deeply low,
When I had reached my destination, he gazed into my eyes,
From that moment our hearts were aglow.

Amanda Jane Martin

CONCLAVE

Grim the faces round the table
in the candle's meagre light.

Heads that nod in solemn gesture
as the plotters all unite.

Whispered formulas were uttered
hands in secret gesture raised.

'Ostracise her' cried their leader
'for she knows our secret ways.'

'She hath knowledge' said another
'of the way our craft we ply.'

'How our prayers are interspersed
with scandal and with lie.'

'Who will rid us of this torment?'
chorused all with one accord.

'Lest upon our blest committees
she has chance to have a word.'

Janet Cavill

FAMOUS QUESTIONS

Is Cilla Black, or Barry White
Can Edward Lear at girls all night
Does Ruby Wax or John Wayne
Is Eric Idle, or insane

Who pays Pat Cash, who paid Roger Moore
Would David Steele if he were poor
Does Gareth Hunt or Michael Fish
Can Richard Stilgoe (if that's his wish)

Is Arthur English, or Dawn French
Does Lyle Lovett across the bench
Can Robin Cook or Steven Fry
Who called Garribaldi (and made him cry)

Was Anthony Blunt and is Tom Sharpe
Can Charles Dance in the park
Is Claire Short or Shelley Long
When Samuel Pepys is he wrong

Is Robert Browning or Quintin Crisp
Does John Speke with a lisp
If hospitalised will Epicurus
Famous questions here before us.

Trev Coope

82 NOT OUT

When you're feeling low just think of these
A list of lies - no need for pleas
Just think when read they could be you
Don't worry you're safe . . . no one ever knew

Whether out with Shirley or the girls
Or back at nan's with all her curls
I'm at a mate's, or her's next door
Just as long that you did score

In a meeting, or at the school
Don't call again, you stupid fool
Can't stay late, someone might see
Those twitching curtains watched her flee

Stay on the stairs, now then be good
Mommy's busy where friends once stood
It's all a game for you she said
That endless book you must have read

How easy yet how sad it feels
To try and win they dig their heels
What self-same scheme will next be tried?
Who cares what said, That love had died

So in the mind of restless man
Happiness from a careful plan
Keeping all those thoughts afloat
Important? Yes. A parting note.

Paul Davis

ECCLESIASTICUS
(not to be confused with Book of Ecclesiastes)

Philosophers say mortal man
hops like a toad across a scree
from stone to stone - and sometimes can
misplace his foot. Such misery
may well result in effluence
of self-condoling eloquence.

Crack'd, drunken chimney pots await
the coming of the man below -
gale-driven, to his shining pate
like homing pigeons, down they go.
His words are terse! he does not shirk
to vilify the builders' work!

Like the proverbial Trooper lies
the *'welcome'* mat on polished floor.
The Suitor takes one step - then flies
(with flowers) through glassy inner door.
(Which sad even appears to show
the pa(i)n(e)s poor lovers undergo).

> *Misfortune dogs the human race*
> *until - bereft of health and vigour -*
> *in Marvell's 'fine and private place'*
> *we hibernate 'in mortis rigor'.*

> *Ecclesiasticus xxvi:vi (Knox Version) -*
> *Pottery is tried in the furnace,*
> *Man in the crucible of suffering.*

W P Flynn

DEAR CASSIE

Cassie (dog)

To return a present, I know is rude,
Especially at Christmas, festive mood,
But for these treats I did not care,
So please enjoy, and with me share.

My teeth and taste now rather jaded,
But younger are you, so more upgraded.
Forgive then please, and next we meet
Forget the incident, you can chase, and I'll retreat.

For Cassie you know as my cousin I care,
But don't push your luck, just don't you dare!
Bonnie (cat)

Grace Wade

HECTIC HOLIDAYS

Hands are busy, heads are dizzy;
All is happening in a rush.
Everybody's in a tizzy.
Cheeks are pinked with happy flush.

Clothes are stacked then quickly packed
As bulging cases start to gape.
Labels loosened from their bindings
Will be stuck with sticky tape.

Cool cotton frocks and ankle socks
Will fit into the haversacks.
Jackets must be neatly folded,
Then come sweaters, coats and slacks.

Bring plenty of that suntan cream
And boxes of Immodium.
If it's hot, we'll need the lot.
To sunstroke we will not succumb.

Don't forget the new prescription,
Though the writing is a tease.
All those convoluted squiggles
Seem to be in Japanese.

Like coolies toting heavy loads,
We try to balance all our stuff.
I think we need another case.
Just put it there. Now that's enough.

The passports, visas, currency
Are safe, so now we can begin
To set out on our holiday.
Please give me one more aspirin.

Long, lazy days with time to gaze
At rural beauties of the Loire,
And should a light descend at night,
Perhaps we'll catch a falling star.

Celia G Thomas

An Alternative Pussycat

Pussycat, Pussycat, where have you been?
I've been to London, the sights I have seen.
Pussycat, Pussycat, that was so far!
I would have gone further but I crashed your car.
Pussycat, Pussycat, you don't mean the Merc?
It wasn't my fault, it was some stupid burk.
Pussycat, Pussycat, what did you do there?
I ate all the pigeons from Trafalgar Square.
Pussycat, Pussycat, what else did you do?
I let all the animals out of the zoo.
Pussycat, Pussycat, did they catch them again?
The cheetah was caught speeding in the bus lane.
Pussycat, Pussycat, what happened then?
The lions got hungry and ate-up three men.
Pussycat, Pussycat, did you break any law?
I picked a man's pocket with my dainty paw.
Pussycat, Pussycat, what did you get?
Six months probation and a jab from the vet.
Pussycat, Pussycat, did he cause you harm?
I got my own back when I bit his arm.
Pussycat, Pussycat, where did you sleep?
In a room at the Ritz, with beds soft and deep.
Pussycat, Pussycat, what did you eat?
Salmon and pate and the tastiest meat.
Pussycat, Pussycat, paying must have been hard.
Not really, you see I had your credit card.
Pussycat, Pussycat, don't leave me again.
I'm gone if it's sunny, I'll stay if it's rain.
Pussycat, Pussycat, will you do this anymore?
As long as there's a cat flap in the front door.

Elizabeth Black

MISS DIRECTED

Oh Doctor please help
Can't think what's the matter
Doc sat in his chair
Fingers locked heard my patter
He examined my elbows
My tongue, head and eyes
My tummy and wrists
My nose, neck and thighs
Said thank you Miss Peabody
There is none to compare
But you're in the wrong office
Doctor's surgery's upstairs!

J Howling Smith

THE PROMISCUOUS PRAWN

Oh one shouldn't pour scorn on the thought of a prawn,
being the promiscuous type

Why most creatures in life will take more than one wife,
without ceremonial hype

So the prawn it is said can be quite good in bed,
though can be stopped by a raging headache

But nine times out of ten he'll be asked back again,
And it's not for the coffee he makes

Well this elegant chap doesn't have to bait traps,
to capture 'la femme' in his life

With style and panache to his side they all dash,
all hoping to become his wife

Now think to yourself with all his sexual wealth,
what more can this conqueror crave

Well a car or a coat or a voice in his throat,
or maybe a night at a rave

No what he wants most and to that he would boast,
the success rate though makes him feel blue

It's not wealth or fame, not even winning a game,
but not to end up as a prawn vindaloo.

Steve Burnett

ARISE ON TIME

While the clocks are forever turning
We sleep, never at all learning
As it ticks merrily away
Being late for work this day
Our brain is tired from the night before
All that walking around, what a chore
Yet we often push ourselves for more
Constantly opening and shutting he door
Body in a complete and still state
Then wake up more on your plate
It's nice and warm time to relax
Like a body in molten wax
Arising time it's warm and neat
Only the odd occasion with resting feet
Alarm set for that unearthly hour
Up and ready to warm with a shower
Grab coffee or tea to chill down
Still not dressed in your gown
If only one could rely on our brain clock
So we avoid work late, not back in the dock
It's not what one might imagine, a crime
Just as long as we can, arise on time.

Anthony Higgins

NO RIGHT EAR

'You've no right 'ere,'
The Jobsworth said, whatever that implied.
But he must have got it wrong, I fear,
Or else, perhaps, he lied.
Because when I felt about my head
I'd still got one each side.
(Ears, that is.)

R L Cooper

COME OUR WAY

Sat in my office
One Monday
The lawyers did say.

'You have just acquired
Two limousines,' they say
'One will have to come our way.'

Take it from me
They would not be good enough
For runabouts truly
Clapped out, they thought
Not, convinced there was
Big cash about.

Phoned back the following
Day and said 'OK'
'Which do you want?
It's all the same to me
Two backs or two fronts,
The lot if you want.'

I could feel their dismay
Though they were hundreds
Of miles away.

It took a while for the
Penny to drop,
Too close to an acetylene
Gun they had got.

'Now which do you want
To come your way
Halves or the lot?'

A K Chatsworth

SPIRITUAL CURRY

I know that we've all got to die, and I'm really in no hurry.
So when I pass, and breathe my last, where I go, I hope there's *curry,*
Anyone will do, rogan josh, or vindaloo, madras or piping tandoori,
Sat at a table with a pint of Black label all covered in heavenly glory.
There may be wonders to see in my eternity, many a miraculous sight
Lots of angels may murmur, as I wolf down my korma, and let out
a belch of delight,
I'll see cherubs on high, playing harps in the sky, sweet tunes to the
heavenly throng,
After eating dansak I'll relax and lay back, join in with the celestial
sing-song,
Paradise is the place for every good soul, be it Christian, Jew,
Hindustani,
But of that I won't care, they can pull up a chair and get stuck
in with me to Biriani.
And although we're dead, can still eat pitta bread, Bombay duck and
tasty kuchumba,
While hot steaming rice will go down just nice, a really good warm
juicy number,
But wait just a bit, what if I'm not fit? And I go to that place down
below,
There'll be troggs, gnomes and demons, the whole place will be
steaming, a hellish inferno,
Where big bad Satan with his horns will be waiting, to welcome me
to his domain,
By then it won't matter, what I've got on my platter, for I'll never
taste curry again!

Ray Moore

THE LEOPARD'S STRUGGLE (TO TELL HIS TALE)

We lay like leopards in the scorched grass
while the human wildebeest trundled past.

'Come and swat some of these flies for me!'

We were grass-sharks, wild and sleek
quick to spot the weaklings in the beasts.

'Get your feet off that settee . . .!'

We used to find joy in spooking them
in mock runs and threatening postures.

'He keeps throwing stones at me!'

But they were so easily sparked into panic
and we were too bored and hot to run the long pastures.

'It's too late now, it's time for tea . . .'

We no longer need to hunt in order to feed
still instinct persists with the heart of the beast.

'Do you think it would be better in green?'

Somehow, we have a duty to discharge
so for duties sake we chase them down to the trees.

'That smell is back, it isn't me . . .!'

I must admit that we're growing fat in the sun
as middle-age slows us down a shade.

'Will you put that down!'

We're more content to watch them run
now that we're past the prime for what we were made.

'Oh for God's sake!'

N D Potter

ALL THAT GLITTERS . . .

How was I supposed to know?
That all the lemonade was show -
The lovely bottles row by row,
Induced my thirst to 'have a go',
Sadly, as the liquid quenched,
Too late! The 'sample' bottle clenched . . .

Pat Derbyshire

TALES FROM THE DEEP

The crab said to the lobster,
Is it really true,
I've heard a rumour, from a mussel,
That your blood is really blue.

Of course that's right, the lobster said,
Swirling up the sand,
I'm the queen of all the shellfish,
I am really very grand.

Said the scallop to the oyster,
Your looking very fine,
Come and have a dance with me,
We'll have a little wine.

I don't think so, the oyster said,
I must not dance or whirl,
The last time I went out with you.
I lost my little pearl!

Douglas Burns

HUMOUR

I've often been asked - as I journey through life,
Why my sense of humour wasn't rife.
I had learnt in my younger years,
That not everyone can control their fears.
So you see I would try to keep an expressionless face,
And got dubbed with the name of being 'straight-laced'.
Few folk were to know that the mask hid much laughter,
That would have rung merrily, had it reached any rafter.
A word or action could hurt with ease,
So I thought it wiser not to tease.
But it didn't mean I hadn't seen the funnier side,
A thing I always chose very hard to hide.
It certainly paid off, for as one gets older,
And life can appear a little colder.
You can call to mind the fun you've had,
Without making anyone feel really bad.

Betty Green

THE JUDGE

In the courts, I believe, I am seen as naïve passing sentences some
say are puny.
The tabloids all rage and on each leader page, I'm described as a
bit of a loony.
I quite fail to see why they criticised me for the rapist I failed to
convict.
The victim, in court, wore her skirt very short - I saw then how the
poor chap was tricked.
In the next case I heard, an habitual gaolbird had been caught
ransacking a dwelling.
The owner, quite piqued, the felon's ear tweaked, raising a bit of
a swelling.
The robber complained, the police then detained, not him but the
chap he had raided.
My sentence was firm, twelve months was the term, and the robber
went free, legal aided.
I know it's the fashion to sneer at compassion but there's where my
sympathies lie.
Thus I freed a young man, a footballing fan, who had blackened
another chap's eye.
He wore a sad smile at the end of the trial, repentance on public display.
That week at United, a brawl he incited was featured on Match of
the Day.
So many cases my courtroom embraces are complex and rarely
clear-cut.
Yet one I should mention that caught my attention was really quite
open and shut.
One afternoon, a yuppie tycoon charged with fraud and deception.
Came up before me, although I could see he wasn't in need of
correction.
He was clearly top-drawer, no breaker of law this chap with
his old school tie.
Community service I ordered for him - provided the weather
was dry.

David Stevens

CONFLICT OF THOUGHTS

The garden's a pretty sight
Knats are beginning to bite
Flowers perfume on the breeze
I think I'm going to sneeze
Trees waving their gentle leaves
Get the rake, I'll roll up my sleeves
Birds singing all around
Making their marks upon the ground
I wonder if they will let us roam?
I don't care, I'm going home.

Kathleen Johnson

BAYSWATER BALLAD

Oh! to be on Bayswater
Now that May is here,
(For she's a little darling -
And really likes her beer!)
Oh! to be on Bayswater
To hear the artist's snore,
(Culture's so uplifting,
And most of them are poor,)

Oh! to be on Bayswater,
Meet Dennis, Fred and Co.
Artists are all bonkers
But it often doesn't show.
Oh! to be on Bayswater
And view the passing throng.
(They all know what they like, of course -
And want it for a song!)

If you want to be on Bayswater,
Beside the park so green,
Then pay your dues to Westminster,
And come and join the scene.

For there is hope on Bayswater,
(Her pitch is 250)
Just tell her that you're 'Coming back' -
She'll tell you where to go!

Beryl Hope

MY MAD MOGGIE

I'm gonna reveal my secret,
Let the cat out of the bag.

We own a pussy, but I'll not brag.
My mental moggie is up to his tricks
Bouncing about like a cat on hot bricks.
He thinks my leg is a scratching-log.
We're always fighting like cat and dog.
He's been in the kitchen;
My wife will have kittens.
If I catch him, I'll soon have new mittens.
Not room in here to swing a cat;
Not a cat in hell's chance of doing that.
Cat's among the pigeons with just one jump;
You should see the table it's like a dump.
In through the door walks my darling wife;
It's too late to run for my life.

Explain this mess . . . I'll have you hung!
Or has the cat got your tongue!

Paul Corrigan

THE BOY AND THE CHIMNEY SWEEP

A boy climbed up a chimney,
Then got stuck inside and deep;
His parents couldn't shift him,
And so they phoned the sweep.

The sweep looked up the chimney,
Into which he pushed his brush;
He pushed so hard, the little boy
Then shot out with a rush.

Dad ran into the garden
To try to offer aid:
The boy was stuck high on the roof.
Dad phoned the Fire Brigade.

The fire engine then arrived;
Mum's heart was all a-flutter,
Because the boy had slipped, and now
Was hanging from the gutter.

A fireman with a ladder
Brought him safely to the ground;
The sweep rushed up and hugged him,
And then gave him a pound.

'I want to give you something,'
He said, 'I'm very keen -
I've never seen a chimney
That I've swept look quite so clean.'

The boy was very dirty,
But he wasn't really hurt -
Until his mother took the pound,
To buy him a new shirt!

Roger Williams

VIVA ESPAÑA

We've packed our bathing suits and we're heading for the sun
Spains's our destination, that's the place to have some fun.
Our taxi's due in minutes and we're all sat in the hall,
Mum's got her floral frock on and her sunglasses an' all.

Quick, quick, the taxi took too long, we mustn't miss the plane,
Who's got the passports? Oh thank gawd! I feel quite sick again.
Has Willie got his travel pills? Has Susie got her hat?
We don't want any sunstroke, no, we can't have none of that!

So this is Spain - it don't look much, I hope the sun will shine,
Mum hasn't packed her nightie? - No! Tell 'er she can't 'ave mine!
She'll have to borrow Grandma's, 'cos grandma's on 'er own.
It ain't so bad bein' naked when you're sleeping all alone.

Well dinner wasn't bad was it? Them shells were a bit 'ard,
What d'you call 'em? Muscles? What d'you mean - 'discard'
Oh - *m u s s e l s,* I should have left the shell?
Oh gawd, why didn't you tell me? Now I'm gonna suffer hell.

This beach is fab, I've picked me spot and now I'm in the sun -
My back's all red, now I'll turn over to get me front bits done.
There's beautiful white sand, both the kids have gone to play,
The nearest stranger is at very least 2 feet away.

Grandma's in bed today - she says her tummy's not so good,
I told her all-night dancing after prawns and chocolate pud
Would only cause more trouble, but she said that she knew best -
It's just the same when I warned her not to go without her vest!

Still - we've had a smashing holiday, we're brown and fit and rested;
Dad's worried that the Customs man will have his luggage tested;
As usual he's bought too much booze and far too many fags,
I told him to put all the contraband in grandma's bags!

Gwen Stone

KING GEORGIE PORGIE

King Georgie Porgie liked his corgies
chasing round the throne.
But then one corgi chewed the orb
he thought it was a bone.
Said Georgie Porgie to the corgies
'Leave my orb alone!
I'll hit you with my sceptre
if you don't get off my throne.'
The corgies bit, the sceptre hit,
they all began to roll.
Then Georgie Porgie hit so hard
the orb spun up the dome.
The glass came down and split a scroll
and fell about the throne -
Said Georgie Porgie, all alone:
'My kingdom for a bone!'

Rosemary Keith

A POEM

You struggle you write you try to pretend
You are a poet you think your horizons have no end
You read the poems of others your keenness is waning
Are you really clever as thoughts like this are not very sustaining
Lots of paper pencils you have a mountain of poems to rewrite
                                    correct and lengthen
As days speed by you find the publisher has a deadline to keep
There is another poem you have forgotten to rewrite lose no sleep
A positive attitude may bring thoughts anew
To write down on paper of memories you have in mind or maybe
                                    of another kind

At last you have completed your poem
You rush around to think of a title
I will call it a poem not very informative but to me vital
You wait anxiously will my poem be accepted
You think the letter has arrived and dropped through the door
                                    with many more

Now you feel very dejected
Days pass by behold the letter has arrived
With great effort you have strived
Excited my poem will soon be in print
Such luck such gratitude is sufficient

Mabel E Nickholds

INFORMATION

We hope you have enjoyed reading this book - and that you will continue to enjoy it in the coming years.

If you like reading and writing poetry drop us a line, or give us a call, and we'll send you a free information pack.

Write to :-
Anchor Books Information
1-2 Wainman Road
Woodston
Peterborough
PE2 7BU
(01733) 230761